THE BEATLES

FOR VIOLIN DUET

Arranged by Michelle Hynson

ISBN 978-1-4950-8915-2

HAL•LEONARD®

7777 W. BLUEMOUND RD. P.O. BOX 13819 MILWAUKEE, WI 53213

Visit Hal Leonard Online at
www.halleonard.com

4 ALL MY LOVING

6 ALL YOU NEED
   IS LOVE

8 AND I LOVE HER

10 BLACKBIRD

12 CAN'T BUY ME LOVE

14 DAY TRIPPER

16 ELEANOR RIGBY

18 THE FOOL ON
    THE HILL

20 A HARD DAY'S NIGHT

22 HERE COMES
    THE SUN

24 HERE, THERE
    AND EVERYWHERE

26 HEY JUDE

28 I SAW HER
    STANDING THERE

30 I WANT TO HOLD
    YOUR HAND

32 I WILL

34 LET IT BE

36 THE LONG AND
    WINDING ROAD

38 LOVE ME DO

40 LUCY IN THE SKY
    WITH DIAMONDS

42 MICHELLE

44 NORWEGIAN WOOD
    (THIS BIRD HAS
    FLOWN)

46 OB-LA-DI, OB-LA-DA

48 PENNY LANE

50 SHE LOVES YOU

52 SOMETHING

54 TICKET TO RIDE

62 WHEN I'M
    SIXTY-FOUR

56 WITH A LITTLE HELP
    FROM MY FRIENDS

58 YELLOW SUBMARINE

60 YESTERDAY

ALL MY LOVING

VIOLIN

Words and Music by JOHN LENNON
and PAUL McCARTNEY

6

ALL YOU NEED IS LOVE

VIOLIN

Words and Music by JOHN LENNON
and PAUL McCARTNEY

Copyright © 1967 Sony/ATV Music Publishing LLC
Copyright Renewed
This arrangement Copyright © 2017 Sony/ATV Music Publishing LLC
All Rights Administered by Sony/ATV Music Publishing LLC, 424 Church Street, Suite 1200, Nashville, TN 37219
International Copyright Secured   All Rights Reserved

AND I LOVE HER

VIOLIN

Words and Music by JOHN LENNON
and PAUL McCARTNEY

BLACKBIRD

VIOLIN

Words and Music by JOHN LENNON
and PAUL McCARTNEY

CAN'T BUY ME LOVE

VIOLIN

Words and Music by JOHN LENNON
and PAUL McCARTNEY

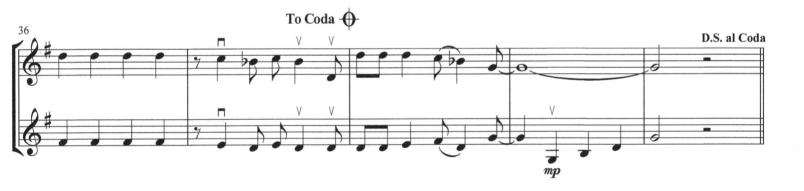

DAY TRIPPER

VIOLIN

Words and Music by JOHN LENNON
and PAUL McCARTNEY

ELEANOR RIGBY

VIOLIN

Words and Music by JOHN LENNON
and PAUL McCARTNEY

Moderately, with a steady beat

THE FOOL ON THE HILL

VIOLIN

Words and Music by JOHN LENNON
and PAUL McCARTNEY

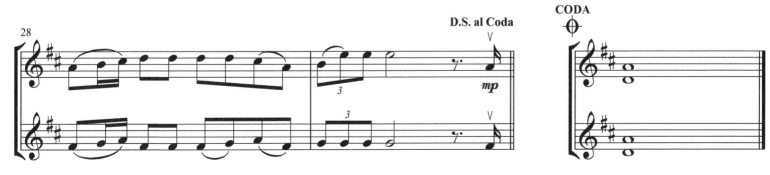

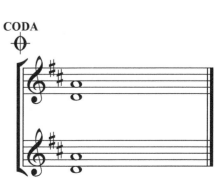

A HARD DAY'S NIGHT

VIOLIN

Words and Music by JOHN LENNON
and PAUL McCARTNEY

HERE COMES THE SUN

VIOLIN

Words and Music by
GEORGE HARRISON

HERE, THERE AND EVERYWHERE

VIOLIN

Words and Music by JOHN LENNON
and PAUL McCARTNEY

HEY JUDE

VIOLIN

Words and Music by JOHN LENNON
and PAUL McCARTNEY

I SAW HER STANDING THERE

VIOLIN

Words and Music by JOHN LENNON
and PAUL McCARTNEY

I WANT TO HOLD YOUR HAND

VIOLIN

Words and Music by JOHN LENNON
and PAUL McCARTNEY

I WILL

VIOLIN

Words and Music by JOHN LENNON
and PAUL McCARTNEY

LET IT BE

VIOLIN

Words and Music by JOHN LENNON
and PAUL McCARTNEY

THE LONG AND WINDING ROAD

VIOLIN

Words and Music by JOHN LENNON
and PAUL McCARTNEY

LOVE ME DO

VIOLIN

Words and Music by JOHN LENNON
and PAUL McCARTNEY

LUCY IN THE SKY WITH DIAMONDS

VIOLIN

Words and Music by JOHN LENNON
and PAUL McCARTNEY

MICHELLE

VIOLIN

Words and Music by JOHN LENNON
and PAUL McCARTNEY

NORWEGIAN WOOD
(This Bird Has Flown)

VIOLIN

Words and Music by JOHN LENNON
and PAUL McCARTNEY

OB-LA-DI, OB-LA-DA

VIOLIN

Words and Music by JOHN LENNON
and PAUL McCARTNEY

PENNY LANE

VIOLIN

Words and Music by JOHN LENNON
and PAUL McCARTNEY

SHE LOVES YOU

VIOLIN

Words and Music by JOHN LENNON
and PAUL McCARTNEY

SOMETHING

VIOLIN

Words and Music by
GEORGE HARRISON

TICKET TO RIDE

VIOLIN

Words and Music by JOHN LENNON
and PAUL McCARTNEY

WITH A LITTLE HELP FROM MY FRIENDS

VIOLIN

Words and Music by JOHN LENNON
and PAUL McCARTNEY

YELLOW SUBMARINE

VIOLIN

Words and Music by JOHN LENNON
and PAUL McCARTNEY

YESTERDAY

VIOLIN

Words and Music by JOHN LENNON
and PAUL McCARTNEY

WHEN I'M SIXTY-FOUR

VIOLIN

Words and Music by JOHN LENNON
and PAUL McCARTNEY

64